POCKET
PRAYERS
FOR HEALING

Other books in the series:

Pocket Celtic Prayers
Compiled by Martin Wallace

Pocket Graces
Compiled by Pam Robertson

Pocket Prayers for Children
Compiled by Christopher Herbert

Pocket Prayers: The Classic Edition
Compiled by Christopher Herbert

Pocket Prayers for Advent and Christmas
Compiled by Jan McFarlane

Pocket Prayers for Commuters
Compiled by Christopher Herbert

Pocket Prayers for Marriage
Compiled by Andrew and Pippa Body

Pocket Prayers for Parents
Compiled by Hamish and Sue Bruce

Pocket Words of Comfort
Compiled by Christopher Herbert

Pocket Prayers for Pilgrims
Compiled by John Pritchard

Pocket Blessings
Compiled by Jan McFarlane

POCKET PRAYERS
FOR HEALING

COMPILED BY
TREVOR LLOYD

CHURCH HOUSE
PUBLISHING

Church House Publishing
Church House
Great Smith Street
London SW1P 3AZ

ISBN 978 0 7151 4309 4

First published 2004 by Church House Publishing

Introduction, compilation and individual prayers © Trevor Lloyd 2004,
2012

Printed in England by Ashford Colour Press Ltd, Fareham, Hants

CONTENTS

HELP, I'M IN HOSPITAL!

Praying for myself

> Heal me, O LORD, and I shall be healed;
> save me, and I shall be saved;
> for you are my praise.

Jeremiah 17.14

Going into hospital is like entering a different world, with a culture we're not used to. And we do this at a time when we have no energy left for making adjustments or for coping with apprehension or naked fear. These prayers put some of those feelings into words directed at God – who is here with us.

Where can we get help? The Lord's Prayer is a good place to start, and this section ends with the Psalmist's answer:

> My help comes from the Lord,
> the maker of heaven and earth.

*

THE LORD'S PRAYER

CONTEMPORARY VERSION

Our Father in heaven,
hallowed be your name,
your kingdom come,
your will be done,
on earth as in heaven.
Give us today our daily bread.
Forgive us our sins
as we forgive those who sin against us.
Lead us not into temptation
but deliver us from evil.
For the kingdom, the power,
and the glory are yours
now and for ever.

*

TRADITIONAL VERSION

Our Father, which art in heaven,
hallowed be thy name;
thy kingdom come;
thy will be done,
in earth as it is in heaven.
Give us this day our daily bread.
And forgive us our trespasses,
as we forgive them that trespass against us.
And lead us not into temptation;
but deliver us from evil.
For thine is the kingdom,
the power and the glory,
for ever and ever.

Jesus our Saviour,
Make yourself known to me
as I enter the hospital.
Help me to adjust to this new manner
    of life.
Give me gratitude for those who care
    for me,
compassion for those in the ward
    with me,
and love for them all.

John Gunstone

*

Lord, I hate hospitals.
I hate the noise.
There is no privacy.
I'm just a back, or a leg or an arm,
And I can make almost no decisions.
But Lord I know absolutely
That I am here for your purpose.
Help me to see you
In the pain and frustration
As well as in the loving care.

Michael Hollings and Etta Gullick

Grant, O God, that amidst all the
discouragements, difficulties and dangers,
distress and darkness of this mortal life,
I may depend on thy mercy, and on this
build my hopes, as on a sure foundation.
Let thine infinite mercy in Christ Jesus
deliver me from despair, both now and
at the hour of death.

Bishop Thomas Wilson (1663–1755)

God almighty,
it's a different world,
coming into hospital.
Give me the strength to adjust
    to being here;
give me patience with strange procedures;
give me love for those around me;
give me some sense of your presence here.
Make me certain that nothing can separate
    me from your love –
neither death nor life
nor anything that happens to me here –
because your love keeps me day by day
in Jesus Christ our Lord.

Trevor Lloyd

*

My loins are filled with searing pain;
there is no health in my flesh.
I am feeble and utterly crushed;
I roar aloud because of the disquiet
     of my heart.
O Lord, you know all my desires
and my sighing is not hidden from you.
My heart is pounding, my strength
     has failed me;
the light of my eyes is gone from me.

Forsake me not, O Lord;
be not far from me, O my God.
Make haste to help me,
O Lord of my salvation.

Psalm 38.7-10,21,22

The Lord is here.
His Spirit is with us.

Common Worship

Lord I can't go to sleep and there is nothing
I want more.

I want to escape from my difficulties and
yet I know that with your strength the
waking time can be most precious, your
God-given time to pray for all those who in
the hours of the night are lost in darkness.
Take this darkness from them so that they
may know your light.

Michael Hollings and Etta Gullick

Thank you, Lord, for being here
   as I wake up.
My eyes are shut, but I can hear
a clatter of dishes: breakfast already?
A murmur of talking: has someone gone
   in the night?
The scrape of a chair: surely not visitors?
A footstep down the ward: coming to me?

Give me peace.
Help me to hang on to you despite the
   distractions.
Open my eyes to face what lies ahead
in the strength of Jesus.

Trevor Lloyd

*

Dear Jesus,
When I woke up this morning my body
    ached all over.
I felt miserable and low in spirit,
Trying to cope with the pain and
    sleeplessness of the night.
I asked you, Jesus, to help me through
    another day.
Thank you that once more, Jesus, you
    heard and answered my prayer.

Diocese of Monmouth Mothers' Union

Is there still a real world out there?
The dawn is breaking, sky brightening,
clouds continually blown into new shapes.
A line of beeches silhouetted on
    the dark hill,
people awake in houses with lights on,
    the start of a normal day.

By the next bed, George's nebulizer hums.
An exhausted nurse at the end of the night
    shift takes my blood pressure.
Another approaches to jab a needle
    in my stomach.
Two buzzers are going, asking for help.
Only four staff on the whole ward.
I hear the jolly tea ladies coming,
And I need space to think.
Does no one else long to stop
    for a minute?

Lord, this is all your world.
These are your people.
Bless them and let them know your
    care today.

Trevor Lloyd

I have no other helper than you,
　　no other father,
I pray to you.
Only you can help me.
My present misery is too great.
Despair grips me, and I am at my wit's end.
O Lord, Creator, Ruler of the World,
　　Father,
I thank you that you have brought
　　me through.
How strong the pain was – but you were
　　stronger.
How deep the fall was – but you were even
　　deeper.
How dark the night was – but you were
　　the noonday sun in it.
You are our father, our mother, our brother,
　　and our friend.

African prayer

Thank you, O God, for all the people who have looked after me today; for all those who visited today; for all the letters and the get-well cards; for the flowers and gifts friends have sent.

I know that sleep is one of the best medicines for both the body and the mind. Help me to sleep tonight.

Into your strong hands I place all the patients in this ward; the night staff on duty tonight; my loved ones, whose names I now mention; myself, with my fears, my worries and my hopes.

Help me to sleep, thinking of you and your promises.

Author unknown

*

The light of God surrounds me,
The love of God enfolds me,
The power of God protects me,
The presence of God watches over me,
Wherever I am, God is.

James Dillet Freeman

At even, ere the sun was set,
the sick, O Lord, around thee lay;
O in what divers pains they met!
O with what joy they went away!

Once more 'tis eventide, and we
oppressed with various ills draw near;
what if thy form we cannot see?
We know and feel that thou art here.

Henry Twells (1823–1900)

Peace to you from God our Father who
hears our cry.
Peace from his Son Jesus Christ whose
death brings healing.
Peace from the Holy Spirit who gives us life
and strength.
The peace of the Lord be always with you.

Common Worship

In darkness and in light,
in trouble and in joy,
help us, heavenly Father,
to trust your love,
to serve your purpose,
and to praise your name;
through Jesus Christ our Lord.

Joint Liturgical Group of Great Britain

THE WORLD OF CARING

Praying for medical staff

> Now there is in Jerusalem near the Sheep Gate
> a pool, which in Aramaic is called Bethesda
> and which is surrounded by five covered
> colonnades. Here a great number of disabled
> people used to lie – the blind, the lame, the
> paralysed. One who was there had been an
> invalid for thirty-eight years. When Jesus saw
> him lying there and learned that he had been
> in this condition for a long time, he asked
> him, 'Do you want to get well?'
>
> John 5.2-6

It's a strange world of desperate emotions, sober
judgements, high-tech procedures, life and death
and love. But God is there in it all, recognized
and unrecognized. Look for him motivating
researchers; breathing wisdom and serenity
into troubled minds; pouring love into those
whose hands reflect his care; bringing peace
to replace anxiety.

Pray for those with difficult decisions to make;
those nearing exhaustion; healers who
themselves need God's healing.

O Lord Jesus Christ,
who alone hast power over life and death,
   over health and sickness,
give power, wisdom, and gentleness
to all thy ministering servants, our doctors
   and nurses,
that always bearing thy Presence with them,
they may not only heal but bless,
and shine as lanterns of hope in the darkest
   hours of distress and fear;
who with the Father and the Holy Ghost
   livest and reignest, ever one God, world
   without end.

Society for the Propagation of the Gospel, 1701

Lord, your touch has still its healing power.
Here are my hands: take them and use
them this day in humble service, so that
your love may flow through them to
someone who needs a human touch.

Sheila King

17

A nurse's prayer

Sometimes Lord, I find it so hard
When people think I am so good,
Caring and loving, because I'm a nurse;
They think I can cope with
Anything
Anybody
Anywhere
Anytime
And that my uniform makes me different.
But on the inside I'm the same,
I have fears that need your love to deal
     with them.
I see pain and death; am I not meant to
     feel?
For that's not love ...
Love feels, and is alongside;
If I'm not feeling how can I show
     I really care?
Help me to show I care in all I do and say;
Lord, live through me
That I may show Jesus to my patients
     and colleagues.

Author unknown

Good Lord deliver us:
A prayer for physicians

From inability to let well alone, from too
much zeal for the new and contempt for
what is old, from putting knowledge before
wisdom, science before art and cleverness
before common sense, from treating
patients as cases and from making the
cure of the disease more grievous than
the endurance of the same, good Lord
deliver us.

*Sir Robert Hutchison (1871–1960),
President of the Royal College of Physicians*

Give to my eyes
light to see those in need.
Give to my heart
compassion and understanding.
Give to my mind
knowledge and wisdom.
Give to my hands
skill and tenderness.
Give to my ears
the ability to listen.
Give to me Lord
strength for this selfless service
and enable me to bring joy
to the lives of those I serve.

Author unknown

O God, who through the healing touch of thy dear Son didst recover the sick and relieve their pain, grant to us who serve beneath thy Cross [in the Queen Alexandra's Royal Army Nursing Corps] such love towards thee and devotion to our duty that the shadows may pass from those entrusted to our care, their darkness lighten into faith and hope, and thy love bring healing peace, for his sake who was content to suffer for all mankind, even Jesus Christ our Lord.

The Collect of Queen Alexandra's Royal Nursing Corps

✳

Almighty God, Thou hast created the human body with infinite wisdom. Ten thousand times ten thousand organs hast Thou combined in it that act unceasingly and harmoniously to preserve the whole in all its beauty the body which is the envelope of the immortal soul. They are ever acting in perfect order, agreement and accord. Yet, when the frailty of matter or the unbridling of passions deranges this order or interrupts this accord, then forces clash and the body crumbles into the primal dust from which it came.

In Thine Eternal Providence Thou hast chosen me to watch over the life and health of Thy creatures. I am now about to apply myself to the duties of my profession. Support me, Almighty God, in these great labours that they may benefit mankind, for without Thy help not even the least thing will succeed.

Illumine my mind that it recognize what presents itself and that it may comprehend what is absent or hidden. Let it not fail to see what is visible, but do not permit it to arrogate to itself the power to see what cannot be seen, for delicate and indefinite are the bounds of the great art of caring for the lives and health of Thy creatures.

From the Prayer of Maimonides (1135–1204),
a Jewish physician in Egypt

Healing God,
may your energy and power flow
    through me,
giving skill to my hands,
compassion to my heart,
clarity and judgement to my head.
Give me strength to minister
to those who suffer and are in pain,
in the name of Jesus who suffered and
    rose again.

Author unknown

Jesus, you cared for all the sick
who came to you.
I want to care with loving compassion,
to attend to details with gentleness.
But I become weary and impatient,
      angry and abrupt.
It is hard to watch the suffering of someone
      I love,
hard to find the energy for all I must do.
I grow discouraged and resentful.
Let me learn from your life of compassion.
Spirit of healing and comfort,
Be with me in these difficult times.
Teach me to take time for myself,
      to be gentle with my own limits,
      to ask for help from others.
May your grace allow me
      to forgive myself when I fail,
      to let go of my expectations,
      to grieve for all my losses.
Send your healing power to me and the one
      for whom I care.
We trust in your love.

Kathleen Fischer

As the body fights for life
As the mind fights for life
As the soul fights for life
May your healing touch be here.
As the days remain uncertain
As the nights lie dark and long
As dear ones become more precious
May your healing touch be here.
In the days of shadows
in the nights
in all time
may your healing touch bless this one,
may your boundless love know this one,
may your steadfast peace grace this one,
in all ways, in all ways.

Lisa Withrow

O heavenly Father,
we pray for those suffering from diseases
for which there is at present no cure.
Give them the victory of trust and hope,
that they may never lose their faith
in your loving purpose.
Grant your wisdom to all
who are working to discover the causes
of disease,
and the realization that through you
all things are possible.
We ask this in the name of him
who went about doing good
and healing all manner of sickness,
even your Son, Jesus Christ, our Lord.

George Appleton (1902–93)

*

We ask for your guidance
for those who are engaged
in medical research,
that they may persevere
with vision and energy;
and for those who administer
the agencies of health and welfare,
that they may have wisdom
    and compassion.

Lord Jesus Christ, lover of all,
bring healing, bring peace.

Common Order

God of love,
your Son brought healing to the sick
and hope to the despairing.
We pray for all who suffer pain,
who bear the burden of illness,
or who have to undergo an operation.
Give them the comfort and strength
of your presence,
and surround them
with your healing love and power.
May they know the fellowship of Christ
who bore pain and suffering for us,
and at the last won victory over death.

Bless those who share with Christ
a healing ministry,
researchers, doctors, surgeons, nurses.
Use their sympathy and skill
for the relief of suffering, the conquest
    of disease,
and the restoration of health;
and crown all their efforts with
    good success;
through Jesus Christ our Lord.

Common Order

Have mercy on me, Lord, for I am weak;
Lord, heal me, for my bones are racked.
My soul also shakes with terror;
how long, O Lord, how long?
Turn again, O Lord, and deliver my soul;
save me for your loving mercy's sake.
I am weary with my groaning;
every night I drench my pillow
and flood my bed with my tears.
My eyes are wasted with grief
and worn away because of all my enemies.
The Lord has heard my supplication;
the Lord will receive my prayer.

Psalm 6.2-4,6,7,9

Our eyes, Lord, are wasted with grief;
you know we are weary with groaning.
As we remember our death
in the dark emptiness of the night,
have mercy on us and heal us;
forgive us and take away our fear
through the dying and rising of Jesus
your Son.

Common Worship: Pastoral Services

ASKING THE IMPOSSIBLE?

Praying for others

> [People recognized Jesus], and rushed about that
> whole region and began to bring the sick on mats
> to wherever they heard he was. And wherever he
> went, into villages or cities or farms, they laid the
> sick in the market-places, and begged him that
> they might touch even the fringe of his cloak;
> and all who touched it were healed.
>
> Mark 6.55,56

How do you pray for those who are ill? In the
Gospels people brought their friends to Jesus.
Some of them once made a hole in the roof of
a house where Jesus was, to get their friend
in front of him. Think of praying as bringing
people to Jesus. Sometimes it takes time,
effort, and a determination not to give up.

And as you bring them, think about exactly
what it is you want to ask him for. These
prayers may give you some ideas.

Almighty and merciful Father,
help of the helpless, and lifter up
    of the fallen,
look in mercy on all who are oppressed in
    mind, body, or estate.
Comfort and relieve them, according to
    their several necessities;
give them patience under their sufferings,
and a happy issue out of all their afflictions;
for Jesus Christ's sake.

Edward Meyrick Goulburn (1818–97), Dean of Norwich

Lord God, whose Son, Jesus Christ,
understood people's fear and pain before
they spoke of them, we pray for those in
hospital. Surround the frightened with
your tenderness; give strength to those in
pain; hold the weak in your arms of love;
and give hope and patience to those who
are recovering. We ask this through the
same Jesus Christ, our Lord.

Christine McMullen

O Lord, holy Father, creator of the universe, author of its laws, you can bring the dead back to life, and heal those who are sick. We pray for our sick brother that he may feel your hand upon him, renewing his body and refreshing his soul. Show to him the affection in which you hold all your creatures.

Dimma, a seventh-century Irish monk

God our healer,
keep us aware of your presence,
support us with your power,
comfort us with your protection,
give us strength
and establish us in your peace.

A New Zealand Prayer Book

33

God of grace and comfort
enfold *N* with your mercy.
Strengthen her with the shield of faith,
and enable her to accept what is to come;
heal her and bear her pain,
keep her in peace, and fix her heart on you;
through Jesus Christ our Saviour.

A Prayer Book for Australia

Jesus, you knew pain,
you knew the loneliness, the weakness
and the degradation it brings;
you knew the agony.
Jesus, your suffering is the only hope,
the only reconciliation for those who suffer.
Be with *N* as *s/he* grapples with the pains
    s/he suffers now.
Be a promise to *him/her*
that this present suffering will cease;
be the hand that *s/he* can hold;
be present, Saviour, for we need you now.

A New Zealand Prayer Book

For children who are ill

Lord Jesus,
thank you because you know I am ill
and because you are here with me.
Help the doctors and nurses
    to make me better
and help me to be brave
and get strong again.

Lord Jesus,
when I'm hot and sticky
keep me cool.
When my eyes hurt and I can't think
    straight
give me a clear head.
When I don't know what's wrong with me,
and get frightened in the night,
help me to know you are here
and to be sure you love me.

Lord Jesus,
the doctor says my friend has to stay
in bed
and we can't go round to play.
Please look after her and make her
better soon.

For a child who has special needs

Living God, creator of us all,
we thank you for entrusting N
into the special care of N *and* N.
Give them and all who surround them
wisdom and understanding, courage
and patience;
give them grace to put aside fear
and anxiety
and to fulfil your purposes;
fill their hearts with your unfailing love,
that N may grow up secure in giving
and receiving love
and in the enjoyment of your presence,

to enrich our lives and the lives of others
in ways beyond our imagining,
in Jesus Christ our Lord.

Common Worship: Pastoral Services

Anxiety and depression

O Holy Spirit who dost delve into all things,
Even the deep things of God
And the deep things of man,
We pray thee to penetrate the springs
   of personality
Of all who are sick in mind,
To bring them cleansing, healing and unity.
Sanctify all memory, dispel all fear,
Bring them to love thee
With all their mind and will,
That they may be made whole
And glorify thee for ever.
We ask this in the name of him
Who cast out devils and healed men's minds,
Even Jesus Christ our Lord.

George Appleton (1902–93)

The breath of life, O Lord, seems spent.
My body is tense, my mind filled with anxiety,
Yet I have no zest, no energy.
I am helpless to allay my fears;
I am incapable of relaxing my limbs.
Dark thoughts constantly invade my head,
And I have no power to resist them.

Was ever an oak tree buffeted by wind,
As the gales of melancholy now buffet my soul?
Was ever a ship tossed by the waves,
As my soul is now tossed by misery?
Did ever the foundation of a house crumble,
As my own life now crumbles to dust?

Friends no longer want to visit me.
You have driven away my spiritual brethren.
I am now an outcast from your church.
No longer the flowers want to bloom for me.
No longer the trees come into leaf for me.
No longer the birds sing at my window.
My fellow Christians condemn me as
    an idle sinner.
Lord, raise up my soul, revive my body.

Gregory of Nazianzus (c. 329–c. 389)

Jesus, Saviour in storm,
when the waters of the deep are broken up,
when the landmarks are washed away
   or drowned,
come to us across the water.

A New Zealand Prayer Book

Father,
we pray for those
who know the suffering
of total despair:
for the terminally ill
and the grief-stricken;
for the depressed
and for those consumed by guilt;
for those who have lost their faith
in life, in others, in you.
We bring before you
Those who feel totally alone
When faced with fears and pain
That threatens to overwhelm them.

Christine Odell

39

Lord, we pray to you,
Knowing you watch over us.
You not only created our souls and made
    our bodies,
You are the Saviour, Ruler and Guide
    of all people.
You love us so much
That you give us reconciliation and peace.

Be kind to us, Lord;
Help and heal those who are ill,
Cure their diseases;
And raise up those who are depressed.
We glorify your holy Name through
    Jesus Christ,
Your only Son.
By him may power and glory be yours,
In the Holy Spirit,
Now and age after age.

Serapion of Thmuis (fourth century): from 'Euchologium'

Abuse

Jesus, our brother and friend,
look with kindness and compassion
on those who were sexually abused.
You see the lost child within
still crying alone in the darkness
where the hidden wounds of childhood still
        hurt, and make them afraid.
When they feel abandoned, give them hope,
when they feel ashamed, give them comfort,
when they feel unloved, give them faith,
when they feel betrayed, give them peace.
In the power of your resurrection
may love triumph over fear,
light shine in the darkness,
and the long reign of terror be ended.

Tracy Hansen

*

Addiction

O blessed Jesus, you ministered to all who came to you. Look with compassion upon all who through addiction have lost their health and freedom. Restore to them the assurance of your unfailing mercy; remove the fears that attack them; strengthen them in the work of their recovery; and to those who care for them, give patient under-standing and persevering love; for your mercy's sake.

Book of Alternative Services of the Anglican Church of Canada

HEALING AND ANOINTING

> *Are any among you sick? They should call for the elders of the church and have them pray over them, anointing them with oil in the name of the Lord. The prayer of faith will save the sick, and the Lord will raise them up.*
>
> James 5.14,15

James's picture of Christians sending for the church leaders sounds simple. They come; they pray; they lay hands on us and anoint us with oil; and healing follows.

Touch and prayer and expectation lead to something spiritual happening. We do not have to understand it, and the healing may be spiritual and not physical. Resurrection – being raised up – might happen only after death.

Jesus sets before us the hope of the kingdom of God. All that is broken will be bound up in God's healing love. All that is marred by weakness and sin will be transformed by God's reconciling love.

In his humanity, Jesus took on himself our weakness and bore our sins. The Holy Spirit is present in the struggles and groaning of a world subject to decay, bringing to birth the freedom and glory of God's new creation.

It is in this hope that we bring to God our prayers and our penitence, and look to God for the new life of the kingdom.

Common Worship: Pastoral Services

Be with us, Spirit of God;
nothing can separate us from your love.
Breathe on us, breath of God;
fill us with your saving power.
Speak in us, wisdom of God;
bring strength, healing and peace.
The Lord is here.
His Spirit is with us.

Common Worship: Morning and Evening Prayer

Lord, you know we find it difficult to
      admit we're ill;
hard to trust others with our bodies.
You might expect us to send
for the church leaders when we're sick,
but this isn't the first thing we think of.
Make us bolder in what we ask
and give us grace in the end
to accept your healing,
whoever you choose to use;
through Jesus Christ our Lord.

Trevor Lloyd

Almighty God,
you called Luke the physician,
whose praise is in the gospel,
to be an evangelist and physician
    of the soul:
by the grace of the Spirit
and through the wholesome medicine
    of the gospel,
give your Church the same love
    and power to heal;
through Jesus Christ your Son our Lord,
who is alive and reigns with you,
in the unity of the Holy Spirit,
one God, now and for ever.

*Common Worship: adapted from the
Book of Common Prayer, 1662*

God never says
you should have come yesterday.
He never says
you must come again tomorrow.
But today,
if you will hear His voice,
today He will hear you.
He brought light out of darkness,
not out of a lesser light;
He can bring your Summer out of Winter
though you have no Spring.
All occasions invite his mercies,
and all times are his seasons.

John Donne (1573–1631)

We meet in the presence of God
who knows our needs,
hears our cries,
feels our pain,
and heals our wounds.

New Patterns for Worship

Lord Jesus Christ, we are weak
   but you are strong;
we are poor but you are rich;
we are sinful but you forgive;
we are sick but you give health.
Come to us through your Holy Spirit,
So that we may receive all that you plan
   for our healing and wholeness,
And may all the glory and honour come
   back to you.

Our Modern Services, Anglican Church of Kenya

Friend of sinners, you bring hope
in our despair.
Lord, have mercy.
Lord, have mercy.
Healer of the sick, you give strength
in our weakness.
Christ, have mercy.
Christ, have mercy.
Destroyer of evil, you bring life
in our dying.
Lord, have mercy.
Lord, have mercy.

New Patterns for Worship

＊

God of compassion and love,
we offer you all our suffering and pain.
Give us strength to bear our weakness,
healing even when there is no cure,
peace in the midst of turmoil
and love to fill the spaces in our lives.

From the Iona Abbey Worship Book

Blessed are you, sovereign God,
gentle and merciful,
creator of heaven and earth.
Your Word brought light out of darkness,
and daily your Spirit renews the face
    of the earth.
When we turned away from you in sin,
your anointed Son took our nature
and entered our suffering
to bring your healing
to those in weakness and distress.
He broke the power of evil
and set us free from sin and death
that we might become partakers of his glory.
His apostles anointed the sick in your name,
bringing wholeness and joy to a broken world.
By your grace renewed each day
you continue the gifts of healing
    in your Church
that your people may praise your name
    for ever.
By the power of your Spirit
may your blessing rest on ...;
may they be made whole
in body, mind and spirit.
Hear the prayer we offer for all
    your people.

Remember in your mercy those for whom
    we pray:
heal the sick, raise the fallen,
strengthen the fainthearted
and enfold in your love
the fearful and those who have no hope.

Common Worship

In the name of God and trusting in his
    might alone,
receive Christ's healing touch
    to make you whole.

May Christ bring you wholeness of body,
    mind and spirit,
deliver you from every evil,
and give you his peace.

Common Worship

O God of heavenly powers,
Who by the power of your command
Drive away from the bodies of men and
    women all sickness and all infirmity:
Be present in your goodness
To this your servant,
That his weakness may be banished
And his strength recalled;
And his health being therefore restored,
He may bless your holy Name,
Through our Lord Jesus Christ.

Gelasian Sacramentary (seventh century)

Heal me, hands of Jesus,
And search out all my pain;
Restore my hope, remove my fear
And bring me peace again.

Michael Perry (1942–96)

Loving God,
you are merciful and forgiving.
Grant that those who are suffering the
   hurts of the past
may experience your generous love.
Heal their memories, comfort them,
and send them all from here
renewed and hopeful;
in Jesus Christ our Lord.

A Prayer Book for Australia

You, who said,
'Come unto me all you who are weary and
    heavy-laden and I will give you rest,'
I come to you now.
For I am weary indeed.
Mentally and physically I am bone-tired.
I am all wound up, locked up tight
    with tension.
I am too tired to eat.
Too tired to think.
Too tired even to sleep.
I feel close to the point of exhaustion.

Lord, let your healing love flow through me.
I can feel it easing my tensions.
Thank you.
I can feel my body relaxing.
Thank you.
I can feel my mind begin to go calm and
    quiet and composed.
Thank you for unwinding me, Lord,
    for unlocking me.
I am no longer tight and frozen
    with tiredness,
but flowing freely, softly, gently
    into your healing rest.

Marjorie Holmes

Lord Jesus Christ, you are the only source
of health for the living, and you promise
eternal life to the dying. I entrust myself
to your holy will. If you wish me to stay
longer in this world, I pray that you will
heal me of my present sickness. If you wish
me to leave this world, I readily lay aside
this mortal body, in the sure hope of
receiving an immortal body which shall
enjoy everlasting health. I ask only that
you relieve me of pain, that whether I live
or die, I may rest peaceful and contented.

Desiderius Erasmus of Rotterdam (c. 1466–1536)

Thank you Lord for your promise
that a prayer made in faith
will heal a sick person.
Show me what to pray for,
give me faith,
and answer our prayer for N.

Trevor Lloyd

I am praying for my friend who is so
   very ill.
O my Lord, you brought the touch
   of healing
to those who crossed your path
in your earthly life.
You promised to respond to the prayers
of your children that struggle to follow
and reflect you on this earth.
Reach out now to this one with your
   healing touch.
She belongs to you, O God.
She yearns so deeply to serve you.
Restore her to life and wholeness
   once more.
And even while she suffers,
may she sense your nearness
and be embraced by your peace.
Grant that she may have joy
even in the midst of her sufferings.
And grant, blessed Lord,
that she might get well again.

Leslie F. Brandt

Lord, grant your healing grace to all
     who are sick, injured or disabled,
that they may be made whole.

Grant to all who are lonely, anxious
     or depressed
a knowledge of your will and an awareness
     of your presence.

Grant to all who minister to those
     who are suffering
wisdom and skill, sympathy and patience.

Mend broken relationships, and restore
     to those in distress
soundness of mind and serenity of spirit.

Sustain and support those who seek
     your guidance
and lift up all who are brought low
     by the trials of this life.

Grant to the dying peace and a holy death,
and uphold by the grace and consolation
     of your Holy Spirit
     those who are bereaved.

Restore to wholeness whatever is broken
   by human sin,
in our lives, in our nation,
   and in the world.

You are the Lord
   who does mighty wonders.
You have declared your power
   among the peoples.
With you, Lord, is the well of life,
and in your light do we see light.
Hear us, Lord of life,
heal us, and make us whole.

Common Worship: Pastoral Services

Keeping well?

Praying for wholeness

> *Behold, I will bring my people restoration and*
> *health, and I will heal them and draw back the*
> *curtain on an abundance of peace and stability.*

Jeremiah 33.6

> *May the God of peace himself sanctify you*
> *entirely; and may your spirit and soul and body*
> *be kept sound and blameless at the coming of*
> *our Lord Jesus Christ. The one who calls you*
> *is faithful, and he will do this.*

I Thessalonians 5.23,24

*How do you know you're ill? Only because
you have in your mind and body and heart a
pattern of normality, ordinariness, wholeness,
which you have left behind. So explore and
celebrate wholeness, being made in God's image
and being restored in that image, complete one
day in heaven.*

*These prayers might help to move our minds
away from illness, fragmentation and dissolution
into that wholeness which God wants for us as
we think about our expectations of life, living
for now on earth and preparing for heaven.
'Lift up your hearts!'*

*

Bless the Lord, O my soul,
and all that is within me bless
   his holy name.
Bless the Lord, O my soul,
and forget not all his benefits;
Who forgives all your sins
and heals all your infirmities;
Who redeems your life from the Pit
and crowns you with faithful love
   and compassion;
Who satisfies you with good things,
so that your youth is renewed like
   an eagle's.

Psalm 103.1-5

*

It is right to give you thanks
in sickness and in health,
in suffering and in joy,
through Christ our Saviour and
    our Redeemer,
who as the Good Samaritan
tends the wounds of body and spirit.
He stands by us and pours out for
    our healing
the oil of consolation and the wine of
    renewed hope,
turning the darkness of our pain
into the dawning light of his kingdom.
And now we join with saints and angels
for ever praising you and saying:
Holy, holy, holy Lord,
God of power and might,
heaven and earth are full of your glory.
Hosanna in the highest.
To you be glory and praise for ever.

Common Worship: Pastoral Services

Slow me down, Lord. Slow me down!
Ease the pounding of my heart
by the quieting of my mind ...
Give me amid the confusion of my day,
the calmness of the everlasting hills.
Break the tensions of my nerves
    and muscles
with the soothing music
    of the singing streams
that live in my memory.
Help me to know the magical,
restoring power of sleep.
Teach me the art of taking
    one-minute vacations,
of slowing down to look at a flower,
to chat with a friend, to pat a dog,
to read a few lines from a good book.
Remind me each day of the fable
of the hare and the tortoise,
that I may know that the race
is not always to the swift
but that there is more to life
than increasing its speed.
Let me look upward
into the branches of the towering oak

and know that it is great and strong
because it grew slowly and well.
Slow me down, Lord,
and inspire me to send my roots
deep into the soil of life's enduring values
that I may grow toward the stars
of my greater destiny.

Wilfred A. Peterson (1900–51)

Thy way, not mine, O Lord,
however dark it be;
lead me by thine own hand,
choose out the path for me.

Smooth let it be or rough,
it will be still the best;
winding or straight, it leads
right onward to thy rest.

Choose thou for me my friends,
my sickness or my health;
choose thou my cares for me,
my poverty or wealth.

Horatius Bonar (1808–89)

Intimate God,
you are able to accept in us
what we cannot even acknowledge;
you have named in us
what we cannot bear to speak of;
you hold in your memory
what we have tried to forget;
you will hold out to us
a glory we cannot imagine.
Reconcile us through your cross
to all that we have rejected in ourselves,
that we may find no part of your creation
to be alien or strange to us,
and that we ourselves may be made whole,
through Jesus Christ, our lover and
     our friend.

Janet Morley

The Lord is here,
his Spirit is with us.
We need not fear,
his Spirit is with us.
We are surrounded by love,
his Spirit is with us.
We are immersed in peace,
his Spirit is with us.
We rejoice in hope,
his Spirit is with us.
We travel in faith,
his Spirit is with us.

David Adam

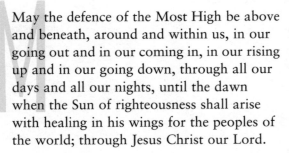

May the defence of the Most High be above
and beneath, around and within us, in our
going out and in our coming in, in our rising
up and in our going down, through all our
days and all our nights, until the dawn
when the Sun of righteousness shall arise
with healing in his wings for the peoples of
the world; through Jesus Christ our Lord.

*The Collect of the Airborne Forces
(including the Parachute Regiment)*

Be the strength of God
between me and each weakness
Be the light of God
between me and each darkness
Be the joy of God
between me and each sadness
Be the calm of God
between me and each madness
Be the life of God
between me and each death
Be the Spirit of God
between me and each breath
Be the love of God
between me and each sigh
Be the Presence of God
with me when I die.

David Adam

Lord of my darkest place:
let in your light.

Lord of my greatest fear:
let in your peace.

Lord of my most bitter shame:
let in your word of grace.

Lord of my oldest grudge:
let in your forgiveness.

Lord of my deepest anger:
let it out.
Lord of my loneliest moment:
let in your presence.

Lord of my truest self – my all:
let in your wholeness.

Alison Pepper

Now we give you thanks
that, taking upon himself our
    human nature,
Jesus shared our joy and our tears,
bore all our sickness,
and carried all our sorrows.
Through death he brought us
to the life of his glorious resurrection,
giving for frailty eternal strength,
and restoring in us the image of
    your glory.

Common Worship: Pastoral Services

O Lord, support us
all the day long of this troublous life,
until the shades lengthen
    and the evening comes,
the busy world is hushed,
the fever of life is over
and our work is done.
Then, Lord, in Thy mercy grant us
    safe lodging,
a holy rest, and peace at the last;
through Jesus Christ our Lord.

John Henry Newman (1801–90)

God the Father, your will for all people is
    health and salvation.
We praise and bless you, Lord.

God the Son,
you came that we might have life,
and might have it more abundantly.
We praise and bless you, Lord.

God the Holy Spirit,
you make our bodies
the temple of your presence.
We praise and bless you, Lord.

Holy Trinity, one God,
in you we live and move and have
    our being.
We praise and bless you, Lord.

Common Worship: Pastoral Services

Lord Jesus Christ,
King of Kings;
You have power over life and death,
You know even that which is not clear,
    but hard to understand;
What I think and feel is not hidden
    from you.
Therefore, cleanse me from my hidden sins,
For you have seen the wrong I have done.

As each day passes,
The end of my life becomes ever nearer,
And my sins increase in number.
You, Lord, my Creator,
    know how feeble I am,
And in my weakness, strengthen me;
When I suffer, uphold me,
And I will glorify you,
My Lord and my God.

Ephraem of Syria (308?–373): from 'Proverbs'

God of the unknown
As age draws in on us, irresistible
    as the tide,
make our life's last quarter the best
    that there has been.
As our strength ebbs, release
    our inner vitality,
all you have taught us over the years;
as our energy diminishes,
increase our compassion, and educate
    our prayer.
You have made us human to share
    your divine life;
grant us the first-fruits;
make our life's last quarter the best
    that there has been.

A New Zealand Prayer Book

Father of all mercies,
for your gifts of healing and forgiveness,
for grace to love and care for one another,
for your hidden blessings,
and for all you have in store for us,
we give you thanks,
through Jesus Christ our Lord.

A Prayer Book for Australia

May God keep you all your days.
May Christ shield you in all your ways.
May the Spirit bring you healing and peace.
May God the Holy Trinity
    drive all darkness from you
and pour upon you blessing and light.

New Patterns for Worship

The Lord God almighty is our Father:
he loves us and tenderly cares for us.
The Lord Jesus Christ is our Saviour:
he has redeemed us and will defend us
    to the end.
The Lord, the Holy Spirit is among us:
he will lead us in God's holy way.
To God almighty, Father, Son,
    and Holy Spirit,
be praise and glory today
    and for ever. Amen.

Trevor Lloyd

INDEX OF FIRST LINES

Now we give you thanks, 69

O blessed Jesus, you ministered to all, 42
O God of heavenly powers, 52
O God, who through the healing touch, 21
O heavenly Father, we pray for those, 27
O Holy Spirit who dost delve into all things, 37
O Lord, holy Father, creator of the universe, 33
O Lord Jesus Christ, who alone hast power, 17
O Lord, support us, 70
Our eyes, Lord, are wasted with grief, 30
Our Father in heaven, 2
Our Father, which art in heaven, 3

Peace to you from God our Father who hears our cry, 15

Slow me down, Lord. Slow me down!, 63
Sometimes Lord, I find it so hard, 18

Thank you, Lord, for being here as I wake up, 9
Thank you Lord for your promise, 55
Thank you, O God, for all the people, 13
The breath of life, O Lord, seems spent, 38
The light of God surrounds me, 14
The Lord God almighty is our Father, 75
The Lord is here, 7
The Lord is here, his Spirit is with us, 66
Thy way, not mine, O Lord, 64

We ask for your guidance, 28
We meet in the presence of God, 47

You, who said, 54

INDEX OF AUTHORS AND SOURCES

ACKNOWLEDGEMENTS

The compiler and publisher gratefully
acknowledge permission to reproduce copyright
material in this anthology. Every effort has been
made to trace and contact copyright holders.
If there are any inadvertent omissions we
apologize to those concerned; please send
any information to the publishers who will
make a full acknowledgement in future editions.

The New Revised Standard Version of the Bible,
Anglicized Edition (NRSV): © 1989, 1995 by
the Division of Christian Education of the
National Council of the Churches of Christ in
the United States of America. All rights reserved
(pp. 1, 16, 31, 43, 59).
Anglican Church in Aotearoa, New Zealand
and Polynesia: copyright material taken from
*A New Zealand Prayer Book – He Karakia
Mihinare O Aotearoa* (1989) and used with
permission (pp. 33, 34, 39, 73).
The Anglican Church of Australia: from
A Prayer Book for Australia, copyright ©
1995 The Anglican Church of Australia Trust
Corporation. All rights reserved (pp. 34, 53, 74).
The Anglican Church of Kenya: from *Our
Modern Services*, Uzima Press, PO Box 48127

Nairobi, copyright © 2002 Anglican Church of Kenya (p. 48).

The Archbishops' Council of the Church of England: *Common Worship: Services and Prayers for the Church of England*; *Common Worship: Pastoral Services* (2000); *Common Worship: Daily Prayer* (2001), *New Patterns for Worship* (2002), all of which are copyright © The Archbishops' Council of the Church of England (pp. 2, 7, 15, 30, 36, 44, 45, 46, 47, 49, 50, 51, 57, 58, 61, 62, 69, 70, 71, 74).

Augsburg Fortress Publishers: reprinted from *Book of Christian Prayers* by Leslie Brandt, copyright © 1974 Augsburg Publishing House. Used by permission of Augsburg Fortress (p. 56).

Permission granted by Heacock Literary Agency, Inc., Cloudcroft, NM, USA, for 'Slow Me Down Lord', from *The Art of Living Treasure Chest*, by Wilfred A. Peterson (Simon and Schuster 1977) (p. 63).

British Medical Journal: from *BMJ* 1953:1:671, copyright © BMJ Publishing Group. Used with permission (p. 19).

Cambridge University Press: Extracts from *The Book of Common Prayer* (1662), the rights in which are vested in the Crown, are reproduced by permission of the Crown's Patentee, Cambridge University Press (pp. 3, 46).

The General Synod of the Anglican Church of Canada: excerpted from *The Book of*

Alternative Services of the Anglican Church of Canada, copyright © 1985 by the General Synod of the Anglican Church of Canada. Used with permission (p. 42).

Hazelden Foundation, Center City, MN: from *The Twelve Step Prayer Book*, copyright © 1990 Hazelden Foundation, reprinted by permission (p. 12).

Healthcare Sunday: from the Healthcare Sunday Resources pack, copyright © 2002 Healthcare Sunday (p. 18).

Highland Books: from John Gunstone, *Prayers for Healing*, copyright © 1987 John Gunstone (p. 4).

The Iona Community: from the *Iona Abbey Worship Book*, copyright © Iona Community, Wild Goose Publications 2001 (p. 49).

The Joint Liturgical Group of Great Britain: from *The Daily Office*, SPCK and Epworth Press, 1968 (p. 15).

The Ven. Trevor Lloyd: copyright © 2004 Trevor Lloyd (pp. 6, 9, 11, 35, 36, 45, 55, 75).

McCrimmon Publishing Co. Ltd, Great Wakering, Essex: from Michael Hollings and Etta Gullick, *It's me, O Lord*, copyright © 1972 McCrimmon Publishing Co. Ltd (pp. 5, 8).

Janet Morley: from *All Desires Known* MOW 1988, SPCK 1992, copyright © Janet Morley (p. 65).

The Mothers' Union, 24 Tufton Street, London

SW1P 3RB: from Rachel Stowe (Compiler), *Women at Prayer; Day by Day Prayers for Every Woman*. Marshall Pickering, 1994, used with kind permission (pp. 10, 17, 32).

Panel on Worship, Church of Scotland: from *Common Order*, 1994, copyright © Panel on Worship, Church of Scotland (pp. 28, 29).

Paulist Press: from Kathleen Fischer and Thomas Hart, *A Counsellor's Prayer Book*, copyright © 1994 Kathleen Fischer and Thomas Hart, in *Prayers for Health and Healing*, SPCK 2000 (p. 25).

Michael Perry: copyright © Mrs B. Perry and Jubilate Hymns (p. 52).

SPCK: from the SPCK collection *Prayers for Health and Healing*, copyright © 2000 SPCK (pp. 13, 25, 26, 39, 54).

SPCK: from George Appleton: *Acts of Devotion* SPCK 1963 (pp. 27, 37).

SPCK: from Michael D. McMullen (ed.), *Clouds of Heaven*, Triangle Books, copyright © 1996 SPCK (pp. 40, 52, 72).

SPCK: from Tracy Hansen, *Seven for a Secret that's Never been Told*, Triangle Books, copyright © 1991 SPCK (p. 41).

SPCK: from David Adam, *Tides and Seasons*, Triangle Books, copyright © 1989 SPCK (pp. 66, 67).

Lois Turley: from the web site *Carenurse.com*, used with permission (p. 20).

Zondervan: prayer by Alison Pepper in Angela
Ashwin, *The Book of a Thousand Prayers*,
copyright © 2003 Zondervan (p. 68).
The Collect of Queen Alexandra's Royal
Nursing Corps and The Collect of the Airborne
Forces (including the Parachute Regiment) from
*The Collects of the Regiments, Departments and
Corps of the British Army* (1996), used by kind
permission of the Ministry of Defence
(Chaplains) Army (pp. 21, 67).

The introductions to each section of the book
are by Trevor Lloyd.